lessons

lessons

Reflections on Early Motherhood

Karen McMillan

Copyright © 2020 Karen McMillan
All rights reserved.

*For all the newborn mothers.
And my mum, Annie.*

CONTENTS

Preface	11
A Quiet War	12
Written All Over Me	13
Where Did They Go?	14
It's Not Going On Your C.V.	16
Problem-Solver	18
The Sun Will Still be Shining	20
The Truth-tellers	22
One Day	24
Constant Nostalgia	26
Boss Babies	27
Her Indoors	28
Stuck Inside a Cloud	30
Never Better	32
Imposter Syndrome	34
Voices in the Dark	36
Sorry	38
We'll be Different	40
I'm so Rubbish at This	42

I Know I'm a Good Mum	44
The Responsible One	47
Right Noise	48
Strange Dance	50
Submission	52
Last Feed	54
All Eyes on Me	56
Sleep At Last	58
Danger Nap	60
Be More Roald	62
Sleep is Coming	64
One Last Fourth Trimester	66
Formative Years	68
The Payoff is Now	70
Grown	71
Always the Postman	72
We Regress Too	74
Fewer Words Lately	76
Tell Me	77
Quiet Acts of Rebellion	78
Oh Come Here!	80
Missing Puzzle Piece	82
The Most Important Work	84

Puddles	86
The Long Game	88
Cross That Bridge	90
No More Tears	92
No Keeping You	94
Just You Wait	95
Acknowledgements	97
About the Author	99

preface

I became a mother overnight.

Yet, in so many ways, I didn't.

It was a slow and often uneasy period of transformation. A gradual goodbye to my old self and an acceptance of my new maternal identity. Or as Dana Raphael, (1973) so brilliantly coins it, my 'Matrescence' (the process of becoming a mother).

What follows is a collection of my thoughts from the first few years of motherhood; a strange time of change, sleeplessness, worry and indescribable love. These are the hard lessons I learned.

So, next time you're having a hard day or are beating yourself up, cut yourself some slack. Remember, this is your matrescence. It may well be replete with growing pains and awkwardness. But it is infinitely worth it.

a quiet war

Oh, how I'd love to go back to those first days and months. I was ever-present, yet never really there at all.

My head was elsewhere. Caught up in all the 'shoulds.' In the baby books, the must-have apps, the impossible schedules; all the perceived perfections of motherhood that felt so at odds with what you were telling me you needed.

I followed my heart every single time. But never with conviction. Always apologetically. As though I were somehow giving in. Not doing it right. I fought it like a quiet war. It was exhausting.

I'd love to go back and mother that version of you, but as this version of me, the mum I am today. More relaxed, more rested, more sure. No longer seeking approval, embracing the fact that I will be happily rocking my boy to sleep until he no longer needs it.

It's not just our babies that grow.

written all over me

Yes, early motherhood was hard and I made it look even harder. It was written all over me. I reeked of it. I sat in my tiredness. I waded through it heavy-boned, like a cautionary tale of how *not* to do this.

And I held the look of a newly born mother for years. The look of someone uncomfortable in her own skin. A rocking, pacing state of constant high alert.

I was always afraid of something. Things that now seem quite trivial; failed naps, rejected meals, public meltdowns. All of the self-prescribed markings of failure.

I'm not sure what exactly took the edge off. Time, I guess. Because, slowly the weight lifted, and the outside world felt like mine again. I could be both myself and a mother.

I can see the beauty in it now; my matrescence in all its awkward glory. The growing pains, the slow unpretty transformation into becoming mum.

And I would do it all again. Because it ended with you.

where did they go?

I used to wonder, what happened to mums when they had a child? Where did they go?

Almost symbolically, they seemed to gradually disappear from their own profile pictures and be replaced instead by baby photos. I don't know why but it used to irk me a bit. I would wonder, how was it possible to get so completely lost in motherhood?

Now I get it.

There *is* a loss of identity when you become a mum. Well, there certainly was for me. You become consumed with all these things that never crossed your mind before; milk intake, nappy output, nap timings, meal plans, teething remedies.

And somewhere along the way, you lose yourself a bit. You forget how to talk about things outside the realm of mothering. You lose touch of the things that used to make you tick. Your repertoire becomes limited and, let's be honest, a little bit dull.

Thankfully, you find other mums; people whom

you maybe wouldn't have got on that well with before, but now you're all rattling around in this lost property box together.

I know deep down that I have gone awol since becoming a mum. I have almost forgotten that there is a world out there, distinct from motherhood, that I can also subscribe to. And share with Casey.

I'm sure he too would like to know the person beyond mum. And so, I am slowly trying to reclaim my Karen-ness. I'm finding, when I do, he actually enjoys it more. It feels more authentic. Just little things, like we'll have a dance around to the music that I love rather than the Wiggles or taking the time to look half-human in the morning and repainting my old face on again.

It can be a balancing act, trying to help this little person develop their identity, whilst not forgetting your own.

it's not going on your c.v.

Do you ever look back at old photos? Them at six months? At 12 months? When you were really in the thick of it with sleep regressions, introducing solids and force-feeding medicine for yet another virus.

Do you ever look at their lovely little face and think, *"How could I not have just enjoyed you more?"*

Why did I get so consumed by the idea of doing a good job, that at times it became just that. A Job. With self-imposed schedules and imagined targets to meet.

Was the world going to implode if he didn't eat or sleep at these set specific times? Who was I even reporting to? Casey? His dad? The health visitor? Was there going to be a probation meeting 12 weeks in, where it would be decided if I got kept on, or politely asked to pack up my things?

When Casey was a year old we were travelling back from Wales on an overcrowded train. Casey was teething and miserable and cried. A lot. I was singing 'Wheels On The Bus' for what felt like hours.

Later on, a lovely older welsh lady came over. She said that she hoped we had ignored the grumpy passengers and that she had wanted to come over and sing along with me. We got chatting and she told me about how she had been a stay-at-home mum for 15 years and really missed those days. She asked if I was enjoying it. Without really thinking, I smiled and politely said: "*Yeah, I love it.*" But something in my face or voice must have betrayed my words and suggested otherwise. Because she quietly leaned in and said:

"Some days are rubbish, aren't they? I used to try so hard. I'd say to myself...Look Cath, it's not going on your CV. That little sentence used to help me a lot."

At the time, I didn't properly appreciate her advice. It's only now, two years in, that I'm beginning to look up and out again. Now, that I can fully grasp those words. Only now that I'm properly starting to enjoy him.

I wish I'd cut myself more slack. I wish I'd skived a bit more and grafted a bit less. I wish I'd taken more duvet days and all the shortcuts. I wish I'd made less bloody pinwheels. But most of all, I wish I'd realised this sooner. Ah, motherhood. If the sleep deprivation doesn't kill you, the mum-guilt will get you in the end.

problem-solver

I was always looking for a reason. A why? There must be some plausible explanation for these never-ending wakeups.

It's the white noise. I didn't buy that flippin sheep. I should have introduced that from day one.

He's too hot. He's too cold. It's these grobags bothering him. He should be wearing socks, that'll be it.

I'm leaving too long a gap before bed. He's overtired. Or could he be under tired? I didn't tire him out enough today. Didn't take him to enough structured activities. He's understimulated. He's overstimulated.

He's not eating enough. He's eating too much. I should be feeding him all those sleep-making foods. Like bananas. Or that magic cherry juice. I need to get my hands on that cherry juice.

Our bedroom layout is all wrong. Bad Feng Shui. It's this house. We need to move house. Tonight!

The bedtime routine isn't solid enough. Did I remember to say goodnight to enough objects around our bedroom? The lamp. I forgot to say goodnight to the lamp.

I should have bought that sleepy scent from Lush. That's where I've been going wrong. Because nobody ever slept before Lush developed that sleepy scent.

Omg, the doubt. The constant second-guessing. I had created issues where there were none. It was bloody exhausting. Almost as exhausting as the actual wakeups. It would be comical, if it didn't nearly tip me over the edge.

So convinced was I that his sleep was abnormal, that there must be some medical explanation, we had appointments with ENT departments for suspected sleep apnoea. But there was nothing. Because he wasn't 'struggling' with his sleep. I was.

He wasn't a code to crack, a problem to solve. He's not what needed fixing. It was me that was broken. Or rather the unrealistic expectations that I held. So very broken.

the sun will still be shining

Certainly for the first year of motherhood, I found it really hard to enjoy those big occasions; the birthdays, Christmas. I would feign enjoyment and buy all the cute outfits, but I wasn't really feeling it.

They seemed to serve as a stark reminder of how much life had changed with a baby in tow. With boobing, napping, eating routines to work around, these occasions felt like extra workload to an already exhausted mum who was waking every two hours. All I really wanted for Christmas was a solid four hours uninterrupted sleep. That was the elusive Christmas gift that money couldn't buy; my Buzz Lightyear doll.

Maybe it's because I'm getting more sleep these days. Or maybe the toddler years are just more fun. But for the first time in ages, I'm finding myself genuinely looking forward.

Early motherhood is often described as akin to being 'in the trenches.' That image is spot on. At times it can feel like a dark, dank, lonely battle where you have complete tunnel vision. But one day, you'll suddenly pop your head above the parapet.

You'll start to look up and out again. And the sun will still be shining for you, and the amazing little life you've created. You'll slowly return to the land of the living. You'll realise that you're no longer faking it but instead enjoying things more than ever before.

And the tired old cliche that 'It's all worth it,' suddenly rings true. Motherhood, it felt impossible. Until it didn't. It's a long game, but one I'm so glad to be playing, now.

the truth-tellers

"It's amazing. You're going to love it."

All those hopeful, well-intentioned platitudes, that we offer up to our pregnant friends. Because it wouldn't be quite right to tell them the whole spectrum of the experience; the good and the bad, would it?

Then the baby is born and the tone changes. The truth-telling begins. After Casey arrived, my inbox was suddenly awash with messages from seasoned mothers. Asking how feeding was going. Admitting how hard they had found breastfeeding and the early days.

It was as though I were being inducted into the real world of motherhood, where the veil was finally lifted and the protective bubble of pregnancy was no more. One friend told me she couldn't remember much of the first six months at all now. She called it self-preservation. I came to understand what she meant by that.

Because I too have forgotten so much of those first few weeks and months. Some of it has become so terribly vague with the passing of the time. But now that I'm through it, I want to remember it all. All of it. I can't even properly remember the first time we took him home.

Moments come back to me in flashes sometimes. His newborn obsession with light fittings, those alert shining deep-brown eyes that reminded me of a woodland creatures. Both arms in the air as he slept. Ah yes they were right, I did love it.

And then come the other sort of memories. Prompted by the smell of a certain brand of nappy bags, the sight of a peri bottle or an out-of-date tube of lansinoh (that is now being used as lip balm) and I balk a bit with the memory of the rawness.

Then I hear news of a friend becoming pregnant.

"It's amazing. You're going to love it," I say.

one day

There's so much I'd like to tell that tired face.

One day, you'll wonder if he's ok because he's slept for longer than two hours in a row.

One day, you'll stop posting in sleep forums for advice. You'll stop scouring the internet for solutions, because you've found the answer within yourself.

One day, he'll let his dad rock him to sleep without screaming. You'll feel redundant but in a good, freeing way. You'll dance around the kitchen in celebration at your new-found sense of freedom, not quite knowing what to do with yourself.

One day, 2.5 years in, he will sleep through the night for the first time, and you'll be really chuffed. But it won't be the all-singing, all-dancing fanfare you've imagined all this time. Because the acceptance came sooner.

One day, you'll catch sight of yourself in the mirror and see a well-rested person staring back at you. The colour having slowly returned to your face.

One day, you'll no longer run on empty but rather a full (ish) tank. You'll start the day with a spring in your step rather than a tired trudge.

One day, you'll think back to those damning conversations and wonder why you ever let them fill your head with doubt.

One day, you'll look back with nothing but pride at the way you responded to your child's needs, in a world that still seems so intent on denying them.

constant nostalgia

I'm scared that I'm starting to forget all the earlier incarnations of you that I thought I never could. The crawling you. The cruising you. The obsessed with pots and pans, you. The you where every other word is perfectly mispronounced.

Is motherhood just a state of constant nostalgia? Of looking back, whilst moving forward. Or do we get to stay still, for a bit, at some point?

I see a photo from just a few months earlier and am floored by how much you've changed. How much we both have. How is it possible to have lived through so many different and distinct epochs in just under three years?

So I write them all down. In an attempt to stop that old thief called time. To hope that the words on a page are enough to capture and retain the feeling. To do it justice without romanticising. Because there's plenty I'd like to forget too. I guess the important things...stay.

boss babies

I have enough contact napping photos to fill a gallery. It felt like such a win when we could finally transfer him to his cot for naps at around ten months. But why? Ten months was still so little in hindsight. I wish I had been less concerned with what every other baby was doing and just enjoyed our reality.

Those early conversations of competitive independence make me cringe now. It's like we were all vying to have the most grown-up boss babies who could change their own nappies.

Something about first-time motherhood renders you terrified of creating bad habits. A feeling that if I concede to this now, he will do this forever. Well, he didn't. In fact, he's stopped napping altogether now and I look back at those moments of enforced rest and closeness with gratitude.

The lessons of first-time motherhood keep repeatedly slapping me in the face.

her indoors

I'm financially dependent on a man. Well, if that's not the scariest of my truths now I see it there in black and white. Except life's not black and white, is it? It's a messy but beautiful, sometimes garish, technicolour.

And Spence is not just a man, he's certainly not *the* man who I'm supposed to be sticking it to, is he? He's not the enemy. He's my person. My best friend since I was 16. The person I've relocated cities for eight times in 20 years in pursuit of his career goals. And not because he's a man. But because out of the two of us he happened to have an ambition that pervaded every aspect of his being. Whilst I did not. I worked a steady stream of HR jobs but it was never a calling.

I appreciate I'm lucky that Spence and his career and the sacrifices we've both made have afforded me the chance to be a stay at home mum. I appreciate that many don't have that choice.

But let's not forget that the work I do at home also affords him the chance to be a dad and pursue his career with limited outside stresses. No rushed nursery drop-offs or pickups. No phonecalls to come away from work due to illness. No time off for half-term. No cooking and cleaning. I sometimes feel like a failed feminist. Her indoors. The obedient housewife. All a bit too 1950s.

I'm not the independent woman that Beyonce sang about. I'm certainly not shattering any glass ceilings. In fact, I'm probably reinforcing a few.

But perhaps me and my person don't need to be a sociopolitical statement. Perhaps we are just Karen and Spence, working together as a team, playing to our own individual strengths in our shared goal of having a family and trying to stay (mostly) sane whilst seeing it through to payday each month.

stuck inside a cloud

I met an earlier version of myself at a toddler group today. A mum of a nine-month-old. She had a certain look in her eye that felt familiar. She sat in her tiredness, the way that I used to, and so I gravitated toward her. I introduced myself and we engaged in small talk.

She soon revealed that her daughter wakes every hour and has since birth. I talked about Casey's wakefulness and she looked visibly relieved, surprised even. She said she'd only met one other mum with a similarly wakeful baby.

Boy did I know that feeling. The isolation of being the one with the non-sleeping baby. The one that felt like other mums only liked to talk to me because it made them feel like they were winning. The one who clearly didn't get the memo on day one at the hospital. The one who came to doubt every decision she ever made or didn't make.

I remembered myself nine months in. Casey growing stronger and more vibrant by the day. And me, depleted in body and soul and feeling detached. Stuck inside a cloud.

I told her she was doing an amazing job and that it's bloody hard. They say you forget the sleep deprivation, just as you forget your pregnancy symptoms and labour pains. I don't think I ever will and I'm now forever attuned to other mums who are currently "in it" and want them to know that they are seen, that their child's sleep is not a reflection on them as a mother and that they will sleep again. Well, in four-hour blocks at least.

never better

When Casey was four weeks old I remember asking a newly acquired mum friend *"Does this get easier?"*

It makes me laugh now that I had deemed her an expert because she had a few weeks up on us. She thoughtfully paused for a moment and said *"It doesn't get easier, just different."*

Oof how she was right. All those leaps and wonder weeks that bled into each other. Punctuated only by teething and illness.

But then, somehow, it did start to get easier in small incremental ways that I didn't really notice at the time.

Suddenly, you're not carrying muslin cloths everywhere because he's stopped bringing up milk. Suddenly, he's stopped dribbling and the bibs get packed away. Suddenly, you've no use for teething granules. Suddenly, your back stops aching so much.

Suddenly, he will play independently for 10 minutes here and there, 20 minutes even. Suddenly, he drops all naps and the day no longer revolves around nap battles and timing everything to a tee. Suddenly, the gro-egg seems redundant. Suddenly, your big jam-packed baby bag consists of just a cup of water and some raisins.

Simultaneous gains and losses.

Babyhood. It lasted an eternity, yet no time at all. I soaked it up and wished it away. I'm glad it's over but miss it beyond belief. It was so hard, yet never better. Ever.

imposter syndrome

I spent far too long looking outside of myself, for how to "be" as a mum.

I remember being in awe in the newborn days as Casey would settle immediately for doctors, nurses and health visitors. They were simply talking to him but somehow commanded his attention and created calm in ways that I couldn't seem to. They were so confident around my son, whilst I wasn't.

I would observe as other mums at the park confidently and empathetically talked to their little ones who could not yet speak. I would borrow their little phrases like 'mummy help you?' and 'gentle hands please.'

I'd consume strangers daily routines and assume they would be a fit for us. They never were. I don't know why I was so insistent on trying to force these alien rhythms rather than embracing our own personal ones, unique to us.

It all served to create this unshakeable feeling of falling short. I was not a natural at this. How could I have had the audacity to think that I'd be good at this? Everybody else seemed cooler, calmer, more collected. Better.

But I had mistaken inexperience for incompetence. I should have just watched my baby instead of everyone else. I should have tuned into just us two. I should have given myself more time to learn the act of mothering, instead of being my own biggest critic.

voices in the dark

If you ever wanted a glimpse into the inner workings of a mother's mind, all you need to do is frequent the online groups and forums where every possible worry or fear is typed out day and night by mothers everywhere.

We lament our 'Fussy Eaters' who hold us as 'Mealtime Hostages.' We desperately seek solutions 'Beyond Sleep Training.' We look for a sense of normalcy from those 'Breastfeeding Beyond Babyhood.'

We will pour out our deepest fears to strangers on the internet, in the hope that we might be made privy to the big secret that will somehow unlock motherhood, so that we can then move up a level or two in terms of easiness.

The secret is that there is no secret. No simple solution. No hidden bypass.

I don't think I ever got any solid concrete advice that actually made my everyday mothering life easier (save for Blippi's toothbrush song. That one worked).

But I guess that's not what we're really seeking from these groups. What we really crave is solidarity; to feel that someone, somewhere is experiencing this motherhood in the same way that we are.

And it's these distant voices in the dark that often provide the reassurances that we can't seem to garner from our real world interactions. The distance and anonymity somehow affording us the courage to be more authentic and vulnerable about the same worries we all have deep down.

I wonder how motherhood would feel if we were all a bit less performative in real life. A little less eager to be seen to be sailing through it. Because how can anyone sail through it really; this wild, uncharted and choppiest of waters.

What if we laid bare our biggest struggles of the moment, in the knowledge that we are all a lot more similar than we think.

sorry

To my older sisters who had their babies whilst I was in my late teens. I'm sorry I was pretty useless. I had no idea. You seemed to have it all under control. Was it as easy as you made it look?

I'm sorry I didn't come over more to hold your babies for you, or to just keep you company. I didn't realise that you might need to be held too. I thought the only way I could help was by buying cutesy gifts which, in hindsight, were wholly impractical.

To my ex-colleagues with children. I'm sorry I didn't recognise how hard it must have been for you having to be all things to all people. I'm sorry I didn't take more of an interest in your children. Sure, I said all the right things when you showed me photos of them. But I wish I had really seen them, and seen *you*.

I'm sorry for those times you got called away to tend to your sick child, that I didn't grab your coat and bag for you and rush you out the door. I'm sorry that my first thought was of all the ways it would inconvenience me. I'm sorry I didn't ply you with copious cups of coffee. I am mortified that I would moan about my bad night of five hours sleep, whilst you saw every hour. I am being suitably punished for that now!

To the woman at Spence's work's Christmas party, over a decade ago. I'm sorry I opened a conversation with that awful line *"What do you do?"* I'm sorry I blustered a bit and didn't really know what to say when you replied that you were "just" a stay at home mum. I'm sorry I didn't pick up on your apologetic, almost embarrassed tone (a tone I recognise all too well in myself now).

I'm sorry I didn't build you up instead and tell you what a hard and important job you do. I want to tell you now that you were the loveliest and most interesting person I spoke to that night. I was in my mid-twenties and feeling lost after moving from city to city and working in a string of temp jobs, feeling unambitious and unimpressive amidst a room of go-getters.

Little did I realise my vocation was waiting for me and that I would want to be "just" like you when I grew up.

we'll be different

Before motherhood, I couldn't imagine feeling anything less than loved up with Spence. And we were never *more* loved up than during my pregnancy. The palpable excitement of this shared adventure to come, that was to be ours alone.

I romanticised it. I would trawl through his childhood photographs and dreamt of us having a mini-him. To my delight we did, in many ways.

We would sit giddily in doctors waiting rooms for my midwife appointments, observing the experienced parents. They looked tired. Bored even. They emitted a general air of 'fed-up-ness.'

"It'll be different with us," I'd say.
"Yeah. Course," he'd reply.

But of course, it wasn't.

We were not immune to the ways in which parenthood would irreversibly change us both. We were not exempt from our relationship sometimes feeling like an ongoing renegotiation of contractual obligations. A battle of who does more. An exercise in one-upmanship.

It is an aching irony, that the very person who made you want to embark on parenthood in the first place, will become at times, in the practice of it, someone who you'll feel completely at odds with. On the opposing sides of *something*.

But, I don't think it's just us. I think it's more common than people let on. I think we had to come undone a bit as a couple, in order to become a family. And I think we're getting better at this. At helping each other out. At remembering that we are a team. Reading each other better. Gauging when the other is spent.

No matter what resentments we've felt, we always end our day sharing anecdotes about Casey. Some funny thing he's said. It will only ever be you that I can share the knowing glances with. No-one else would share in my excitement, as I run up the stairs to tell you that our fussy eater has eaten a banana. You will always be my inside joke and my quiet content. And you are the only person in the world who loves our boy as much as I do.

You are often more adept in the areas where I'm lacking and vice versa. We'll take turns at better displaying patience and light-heartedness when the other can't seem to muster it. And it's in those moments that I realise we were meant to do this together.

i'm so rubbish at this

The phrase that came to define how I spoke to myself for the first two years of motherhood.

For every failed nap attempt.

For every bedtime that took hours, only for him to wake 45 minutes later just as I was finally getting around to making myself some dinner.

For every single night where he woke two-hourly like clockwork.

For every meal that was refused and thrown across the room.

"I'm so rubbish at this."

It was muttered under my breath when I was alone with him. Was sobbed as I would dissolve into Spence's arms of an evening. Was shouted as I would stomp up the stairs. Was frantically typed into online sleep forums. Was spoken down telephone lines to my sisters and parents.

They all responded with the same words; *"Just look at him. He's thriving. The proof is in the pudding."*

But I couldn't see that. All I could see were all the ways in which I was failing. And it was always centred around sleep or food. Two areas that were essentially out of my control.

When speaking to my mum recently, she interjected my ramblings about Casey with "*And how are you?*" Her quiet way of enquiring about my state of mind. *"You seem good,"* she continued.

And I honestly feel good. Like something has lifted. In part because I've relinquished ownership of his wakeups. In so far that I've realised they are not my fault or his. This is normal. It's like I've stopped seeing motherhood as something I need to excel at. As a result I've realised, I'm not rubbish at all. I never was.

i know i'm a good mum

I remember the day vividly. Casey was 12 weeks old. It was the first time I ventured out to a baby group. We were in Scotland, away from our families and I needed to go out and build my village. I just happened to sit down next to Ruth. Her son was two days older than Casey.

We got chatting and it was instantly easy. We realised that we lived just two apartment blocks away. That was decided then. We were to become firm friends. So excited was I to have made a mum friend, I came home and took a smiley photo, sent it to Spence and told him all about my new conquest. I was in a post-date afterglow.

On the surface, Ruth and I had quite different experiences of early motherhood. In terms of returning to work, geographical closeness to family, breastfeeding, weaning choices (things that can be strangely divisive in those early days).

We were very different people in general. Ruth was the confident, practical and positive one, to my reflective and anxious worrier. But none of that mattered. We were unified by being mothers and that was enough. Neither of us had it harder than the other. Just different. There was no walking on eggshells. We would discuss our differences openly and never felt judged, just curious.

Ruth is a decade younger than me but possessed a confidence and ableness that I wish I had now, let alone ten years ago. She was full of gung ho. Always looking onwards to the next stage of motherhood with excitement. Planning her recipes months ahead of weaning. Whereas I was inconvenienced by it; filled with dread about finding time for meal prep and worried about choking. Ever the optimist.

We would laugh that Ruth's son was dressed in proper outfits, whilst I would have kept Casey in babygrows all day long forever if I could have. It was a trivial difference but one that really symbolised our different mothering styles. I always babied Casey whilst Ruth always gently encouraged her boy onto the next stage.

She was always ten steps ahead and I most definitely needed that at the time. In my sleep-deprived haze, she was always keeping me informed of what lay ahead. What vitamins he should be having, essential first aid kit items I would need at certain ages, what groups were happening when; my very own mummy PA.

We would traipse around Dundee, timing our

pram naps together. Those chats and the fresh air got me through so many days, after an awful night's sleep.

Ruth would come out with brilliantly confident statements like "*I know I'm a good mum.*" At first, I was taken aback by such an unapologetic un-british statement but actually how fantastic is that? "*I know I'm a good mum.*" How often do we hear that from mums? Hardly ever. Her confidence wasn't cocky, it was contagious.

We moved back down south just before Casey turned one but we are in touch often, with photo spam of our boys. Still unified by the ups and downs of motherhood.

Ruth, I am so glad I just so happened to pull up a tiny chair next to you that day, and yes, you are a bloody fantastic mum.

the responsible one

I was that protected middle child. I would drift through life, blindly at times, safe in the knowledge that there was always someone more responsible, more 'adultier', looking out for me.

But that all changed overnight when I became a mum. And there was no vetting process, no essential criteria for this, the weightiest of roles. And at 34 I didn't enter into it lightly.

Still, nothing could prepare me for how heavy it would feel at times. Because in becoming a mum, I also became the responsible one.

The prepper. The planner. The instigator of grown-up conversation. The advocate for my little person. The first aider. The risk assessor. Eyes in the back of my head now. Subconsciously guiding little limbs onto inside lanes, away from danger.

I finally said goodbye to the child in me, in order to raise the child in you.

right noise

If you had five minutes with your pregnant self, what would you tell her? What would you quietly whisper in her ear? A helpful tidbit that would set her off in the right direction?

'Psst, Kaz. I know how you enjoy them, but please stop watching all those unrealistic Youtuber mums with their morning routines that will bear absolutely no resemblance to your mothering reality.

You will spend months (and expend the little energy you have) trying to achieve these contrived scenarios that might as well have been directed by Steven Spielberg, for they are pure fantasy.

Surround yourself instead with the right kind of noise. The Pinky McKays. The Carly Grubbs. The Kerry Seckers. The Sarah Ockwell-Smiths. The Raising Ziggys.

They will tell you things you won't want to hear at first. About how hard it is going to be. But they will speak to you much more deeply than anything you ever read on those mainstream apps, that keep telling you all the ways your baby should be behaving. You won't be getting one of those kind of babies. He's what they call velcro. High needs. He's bloody lovely though.

Google the fourth trimester. Google the second-night syndrome. Be gentle with yourself. You're going to love it. And sometimes hate it. You're stronger than you think. I'll see you on the other side.'

strange dance

It's a strange, wild dance; this motherhood of mine. I bend and sway. At the whim of sleep and teeth and moods and amounts of foods consumed.

I can swing from pure elation, to downright despair, in a matter of minutes. The maternal see-saw. Good minutes. Bad minutes. Silent tears. Belly laughs. Deepest darkness and blinding light. I run the gamut of emotions daily. Hourly.

I cry over spilled milk. And burst bin bags. And giant puddles of day-glo wee, timed perfectly to the 'beep beep beep' of dinner's ready. Why does it always come to a crashing crescendo at dinner time?

But then, I am overjoyed that he ate his dinner. Or let me brush his teeth. Or cut his nails.

I am a bath ever on the brink of overflowing, either way.

Oh the extremity of it. There's no middle of the road here. No quiet content.

But there is an inherent magic to it. The chance to turn it all around in any waking moment. Start afresh.

Even the worst days can suddenly dissipate with a smile, or a word, or a clumsily blown kiss. An hour can seem completely blissful just by the sheer absence of the gripes that dictated the hour before. An entirely rubbish day can be transformed by medicinal bedtime cuddles.

The sweet ain't as sweet without the sour.

submission

I'm not the mum that my younger self thought or dreamed I would be. Not the contents of a *Persil* advert. Or the woman confidently spinning all the plates and cleaning them too. I don't have it all. I don't even want it all.

In fact I've become all the things I once turned my nose up at. Sitting him in front of the TV at dinnertime because he somehow eats more that way. Stashing chocolate buttons in the bottom of my buggy to coax him out of the park. Hiding in the kitchen for five minutes peace, eating cold left-over fishfingers.

I thought I would be a stricter mum. I would watch TV shows where parents would struggle to sleep train their children. *"Why can't they just let them cry?"* I would think. All they have to do is march them back to their bedroom, avoid eye contact and keep repeating *"It's bedtime."* Easy!

Pah! I hadn't accounted for how motherhood would *feel* and how much I would totally not want to do that when it came to the crunch. I now want to go and give those parents a big hug.

In many ways, I've not lived up to any of my ideals of motherhood. But those ideals were based only on how I thought motherhood should look and not about how it would feel. And sure, sometimes it might look like total submission, like weakness, like bag-lady chic.

But in many ways, I feel stronger and richer than I ever have, powered by the knowledge that I am his comfort, his source of smiles and giggles. His mum.

last feed

And just like that, after 2.5 years, our breastfeeding journey is over.

Something that came to define my motherhood so much (for better and for worse), is no more. His comfort. My comfort. Often the only trick in my bag of tricks. It saw us through many illnesses, a full set of gnashers, fingers jammed in doors.

Giver of sleep. Taker of sleep. The source of many insecurities on my part. I blamed it for a lot of things; lack of sleep, lack of freedom, his lack of appetite, all the so-called bad habits.

I should have cut it more slack. I should have enjoyed the feeding to sleep, instead of feeling guilty that he would never sleep any other way.

We were down to just overnight feeds and I night weaned over the last week. Something I had avoided and dreaded for so long.

But I needn't have worried. All those fears, all the imagined distraught tears, all the deep breaths and self pep talks were unnecessary, as my sweet boy immediately allayed them. A wee favour to his mum.

Sometimes, it's the things we exhaust ourselves worrying about the most, that never really come to fruition in the way that we fear.

I have wasted so much time thinking about how I would ever stop breastfeeding, that I forgot to enjoy it. And I didn't take nearly enough photos.

The lessons are coming thick and fast.

all eyes on me

There's this strange visibility that seems to accompany motherhood. An imagined feeling of surveillance; that all eyes are on you, even when they are not. It seeps into your daily life and decision-making.

There have been times when I've stopped Casey doing something, and not because I've particularly had a problem with it, but because I've felt like maybe I *should* have a problem with it.

And it's minor things too. Like making a big mess at dinner time. Or picking berries and flowers. Or jumping on the couch. I'll go to stop him, whilst simultaneously thinking "*Actually, I'm ok with this.*" But still, I worry that if I concede now to the berry picking, then I'm somehow setting him up for a life of crime!

And I think the doubt stems from not quite knowing where I sit on the spectrum of parenting, from more traditional to all-out gentle. I think I'd describe myself as a would-be gentle parent (but could do better).

In the early days, the gentle approach felt easier because the answer was always simply boob. But when he hit toddlerdom, it became trickier, and the gentle approach didn't always feel so instinctive. I'd bite my tongue but still the words *"share, share, share"* fell from my mouth hourly.

There have been times that I've questioned every phrase that comes out of my mouth, for fear that a certain word will negatively impact his entire future.

Am I praising him too much? They say I shouldn't praise. But still the words *"well done"* feel so instinctively right to me, and make him light up in such a way that they can't be that wrong, can they?

I think I hit peak over-thinking mode when I googled *"Why am I not supposed to say 'be careful' again?"*

And I understand the reasoning behind it. Admire it even. I write the suggested alternative phrases down on lists but they never come to me in the moment. And so I revert back to *"well done"* and *"share"* and *"be careful"* and accept that I will never be the truly gentle parent that I aspire to be.

Is motherhood supposed to feel this scripted and rehearsed at times? Inauthentically reading lines written by somebody else. I wonder if I will ever feel qualified enough to write my own.

sleep at last

He did it! Our boy slept through the night for the first time. Not one single wake-up. 12 blissful hours of uninterrupted sleep. Not at three months as I had initially hoped, or 12 months or even 24 months but at 2.5 years. YEARS.

If you're currently in the thick of it with sleep deprivation, this news might be equal parts terrifying and hopeful. I hope that it's the latter.

I will never forget the lows of sleep deprivation. In fact, all I need to do is type my name into sleep chatrooms (the online forums that saved my sanity, not because they offered solutions but because they offered solidarity).

Here are some of the things I typed in when at my lowest points:

"My nine month old is waking every hour and fighting every nap. I feel like a failure of a mum. I honestly think the harder I try, the worse things get."

"When does this get better?! 14 months of two hourly wake-ups is starting to get to me (it was every hour last night). Every other bugger I meet has these magical sleeping babies. I'd just like to feel like a functioning mum during the day... wouldn't we all?"

"I'm starting to feel pretty anxious and guilty about the fact I feed my 15 month old to sleep and boob is the only thing that will settle him when he wakes. The thought of nightweaning him fills me with absolute DREAD."

"So, what I thought was the 18 month regression was in fact me living my best life. Turns out THIS is the regression. Waking every 45 minutes and only sleeping on my chest. If this child regresses any more he will be back in utero or a mere twinkle in his Dad's eye."

"I feel like I've spent all day trying to get my 20 month old to nap. He's got a cold and is teething and could really use the rest. Admitting defeat now. I'm so shit at this."

To anyone having similar thoughts; you are not a 'failure', you are not 'shit.' I see you. I was you. It gets better. You *will* return to the land of the living.

danger nap

You stopped napping six months ago. But yesterday, out of the blue, after an all-consuming tantrum, you fell asleep on me at 4pm. This was beyond a danger nap. Catastrophic!

Initially, I tried to rouse you. But my efforts were half-hearted. Because it felt like a gift. This daytime cuddle that I didn't realise I had missed so much. So I submitted instead. I sank lower down into the couch and breathed you in. As though it were the last time. Because there will be a last time for everything.

You seem to be edging out of toddlerhood all of a sudden. A little boy now. The baby in you is leaving. Your face has changed so much, but somehow not at all. You're twice the size, but somehow don't feel any heavier.

My mind raced to all the 'shoulds'. *"I should be making dinner,"* I thought. *"Bedtime's going to be so late."*

I thought of all those articles that push the importance of a consistent bedtime. Then I thought too, about how the constant quest for routine drove me routinely mad in the early days. And so I let go of my weird fixation with the 7.30pm bedtime.

You woke as daddy came through the door. We all ate spaghetti together. Then we danced about the living room, to 90s R&B, in an effort to tire you out. We saved ourselves the stress of a long-drawn-out bedtime and you went to bed the same time as us.

It felt forbidden. I felt momentarily like a bad mum somehow. But mostly like a happy one. Maybe, I'm finally starting to relax into this motherhood gig.

be more roald

I've been taking this parenting gig far too seriously. In the early days, I had this absurd sense that Casey was on loan from the hospital and that in order to prove myself a worthy mother, I had to adhere to a strict but ultimately imagined framework of rules around sleep, food and routine.

My motherhood was severely lacking in fun. It had become a performance in doing it 'right'. But I've slowly come to realise that, I'm the parent here. Not bloody google. I can make and break my own rules. I can offer him a bowl of cereal after a refused dinner. I can keep him up later than deemed acceptable.

Why has it taken so long for me to inject myself into my own motherhood? Why have I not seized that autonomy long before now?

I read once, that Roald Dahl would wake his kids up in the middle of the night and pile them into the car – which was full of hot chocolate and cookies – and drive them up the road to the English countryside where they lived. They would walk into the woods, in their pyjamas, to look for badgers. Be. More. Roald

It's true, the best memories I have are of the things that break from routine; the midnight feasts, going to the cinema on a school-night, when we should have been in bed, sleeping on the balcony with my sister, staking out the neighbour's activities.

And yeah, maybe children do 'thrive on routine' but perhaps it's also possible that their little hearts soar on the extraordinary.

sleep is coming

Here's to the often overlooked mums with wakeful toddlers. Still waking every hour or two.

The ones for whom the fourth trimester seems to have spilled out into the 5th, 6th, or more like 10th.

The ones with an eternal newborn, whose very immediate need for you has never let up.

The ones for whom the nights are still as challenging as they were way back on day one, whilst the days grow ever-challenging too with the added dimension of toddlerness.

The ones who feel guilty that they are still not enjoying it as they should. The ones for whom sympathy waned long ago.

The ones who no longer discuss 'how their night was' at baby groups.

The ones who are looked upon as lazy if they nap when baby naps, because, well, he's not a baby anymore.

The ones who 'really should have sorted this out by now.'

The ones whose tiredness has accumulated over months and years, so that it is now just part of them.

The ones who feel like the world has passed them by and that they will never find their way out of this sleep-deprived fog.

Sleep is coming for you soon.

one last fourth trimester

This was the summer that we got to become your entire world once again, your dad and I.

One last fourth trimester.

The three of us adrift together in new uncharted territory but with that old familiar survivalist mentality; one day at a time.

Except this time around, we know you. And we know ourselves a bit better as parents. This time, we're not frantically googling overactive letdown, silent reflux and wonder weeks.

But there are new fears, new unknowns, new questions; mostly from you: *"When can I go to Luna's house?"* or *"When's this bug going away mummy?"*

There are no siblings for you to laugh and argue your way through this with. And so we became your parents and your best pals. Your protectors and your playmates. We learned how to properly play again. Your teddies took on a life of their own. Music became our medicine. The mundane became magical. Comfort became king.

TV time increased ten million fold. Life became slower, more lax. Caution thrown to the wind. Bickering has ramped up, but so too have swift apologies and olive branches. Perspectives having been gained and gratitudes realised.

This was supposed to be the summer of gearing you up ready for starting nursery in September. Of increased toddler groups and playdates in an attempt to prepare you for the outside world. Now it's hard to say what that world will even look like.

And so we return to our bubble. One day at a time. Grateful for this chance to be your everything for a little bit longer.

formative years

There's this mum that I see most days when we go for our socially-distanced walk around the block. I admire her from afar as she wrestles a pram, energetic toddler and mahoosive dog, seemingly with ease.

She's always smiling and inventing little games for her toddler: *"Race you to that lamppost," "You chase me to this tree now," "Oh brilliant you've found a tickle stick," "Quick there's a dandelion. Make a wish!"*

And I smile too, because I see myself in her a bit. I see all mothers in her. Tired but smiling. Trying to wring every last drop of fun out of these repetitive walks around the block.

All too aware of our role as memory-maker. Phrases like 'formative years,' 'time of their lives' and 'only 18 summers' ringing in our ears. You could falter under the weight of it, at times I do.

I have felt such guilt at Casey being an only child during this pandemic, with just his boring old Mum and Dad for company.

I forget too easy that it's often the everyday, mediocre parts of life that hold the most magic for our children, like the races to the lamppost and the dandelion wishes.

Instead of worrying about all the ways I can manufacture "fun," I could just actually start having fun. Real fun. Doing the things I enjoy alongside Casey.

And it feels selfish to say that, but it shouldn't. Because I too have a stake in this little life of ours. Family is the opposite of a zero sum game. My happiness begets his happiness and so on, and so on. It's taken me far too long to learn that. Perhaps these are my formative years too.

the payoff is now

We thought he would forever be a mummy's boy. I felt your frustrations as a Dad in those first few years, when it seemed like only mummy would do. Wanting to give me a much-needed break. Being screamed at during attempted bedtimes.

If my parenthood has been a sudden thrust into all-consuming relentlessness, yours has been a slow-burning persistence. Of putting in the legwork but often playing second fiddle.

But the payoff is now. Because something has changed lately. He calls for you in the night and first thing in the morning. He prefers your bedtime stories. He reserves his biggest smiles for you.

And so, it is me that sits on the sidelines now, looking in at you both with a full heart and a nose slightly bent out of joint. Maybe this is the first stage of losing you to the world.

grown

Whilst the world stopped a while, *you*, my love, did not.

You grew up, whilst we all locked down.

Transforming from baby-faced toddler to our chatty little boy, in the space of mere months. Full of conversation and questions. You chew my ear off now, making me laugh with grown-up words like *'hydrate'* and *'priority.'*

We finally packed away your highchair. And your stroller. The last remnants of babyhood. From today, you now wear pants!

Where once you toddled with shaky-knees, you now stroll arms-swinging. You bound around. I reckon you could take on the big kids slide once this bug goes away. I reckon I'll probably let you.

They were right; childhood waits for no-one or no thing.

always the postman

To the mum without a village. The mum who started a family, whilst living away from her own.

I know how entirely alone you feel at times. How you crave an extra pair of hands. A friendly face. A casual cuppa and a chat. A knock on the door that isn't the postman.

There are no date nights. No brief reprieves. Your partner, and your partner alone, is your entire village. Liable at times to bend and break.

As lockdown draws to a close, you wonder what's really changed, as you look on enviously at these distanced doorstep reunions.

But you will find a strength in yourself that you never knew existed. A self-reliance. The ability to strike up conversations with strangers, in the hope that they too might be looking for their next best friend.

And one day, it will all change, with one genuine connection. The beginnings of something. A telephone number exchanged. An ease of conversation. A common ground. The ability to be yourself. Comfy chats in messy homes.

A favour bravely asked. A favour returned. An 'In case of emergency.' A familiar house nearby that your child knows the directions to.

You are not alone in your aloneness.

There are loads of us. That followed the partner. Or followed the job. Whose hearts will always partially belong elsewhere.

we regress too

Look who's talking too.

That is how I imagined potty training. I expected to be mildly inconvenienced for maybe a week whilst reworking the lyrics to Beastie Boys songs.

I did not anticipate that it would make me cry. It's just wee and poo for God's sake. But somehow, in my head, it's blown up into this massive important deal.

I had mistakenly taken it on as a personal project. The last big hurdle of early motherhood, that would mean I had passed in some way, if I could just crack this before he starts nursery in September.

I thought I was beyond all this now. The caring what people think. But those old habits are creeping back. The posting for advice on mum groups. Asking everyone I know how they did it, then feeling bamboozled when it all seems so contradictory. And Casey, of course, isn't playing ball.

And it has brought all those old feelings of inadequacy back to the surface. The same ones that accompanied the wakeful nights and weaning onto solids. The feeling of doing everything wrong, and that this will never end. That we will never get the hang of this.

I've come to learn that we as mothers regress too sometimes. Back to those early wobbly days. We too require a bit more hand-holding.

Casey could feel that I was emotionally invested in it and was fighting it more. So I'm trying to play it cool, in the hope that once I distance myself from the responsibility of it all, it might somehow become a bit easier.

This has proven to be the case with so many aspects of motherhood.

fewer words lately

Newly born mother. You have fewer words lately. In spite of the many thoughts that spin around your head.

Thoughts about how different life is now. How everything changed. In an instant. In wonderful ways. In scary ways. In wholly unexpected ways.

And how different it all is. Everything. You. Him. Your own face even. A face that has now seen the long days and the longer nights. Even your own bed seems different now, an out-of-reach unattainable place.

And the world goes on turning. And you view it off-kilter for a while. All askew. Like a surreal painting that you'll one day step back into.

And step back you will. And life will be good. Only you'll have more words this time. Too much for some. But plenty and much-needed for all those newborn mothers with fewer words lately, and a vacant look in their eye.

tell me

Casey has reached that age where he wants to hear about the day he was born.

"Tell me," he asks, as I rock him to sleep. And so I begin: *"You were born on the Fourth of June. It was a Sunday."*

And I gloss over the gory bits of course. The parts I choose to forget. They flash up in mind and I squash them down.

"Mummys waters broke at 8am. Daddy panicked and started hoovering and somehow managed to break the hoover." He likes that part. I give him the comedy, the palatable version, whilst secretly remembering and feeling the whole spectrum of the experience.

And it strikes me that my birth story is much like my mother story. There is both magic and terror. That beautiful, messy mixture of overlaying best and worst. There are the parts we gloss over. And the parts we choose to forget.

But it is infinitely worth it, for the child in your arms saying, *"Tell me."*

quiet acts of rebellion

It took becoming a mum, for me to finally find my rebellious side. I've been described as 'nice' and 'inoffensive' my whole life.

But with motherhood came a realisation, an awakening. Because as much as I love being his mum, I'm not so enamoured by the institution of motherhood.

And I've discovered that I'm not so good at following its rules. Or its books. But what I once saw as failure, was in fact failure to comply to an imagined framework of impossible ideals written by somebody else.

So, forgive me, but I will feed to sleep. I will rock to sleep. I will (god forbid) indulge in eye-contact with my child at bedtime. I will embrace the danger nap. I will skip a bath tonight if we are both beyond it. I will let go of 'he should be doing this by now.'

I will stop beating myself up for not having arts and crafts available at every turn. I will let him get bored occasionally. I will let him snack just before meals to avoid the mother of all meltdowns.

I will choose my battles. I will buy the shop-bought cake. I will incorporate 'lazy' moments into the course of our day, so that I am not left spent by the end of it. I will proudly say I am a stay at home mum. And lose the 'just.'

I now revel in these quiet acts of rebellion; with the knowledge that he is fed, he is loved, he is safe.

And I am sane.

oh come here!

When I night-weaned Casey six months ago, I swapped a rod for a rod, and started rocking him to sleep instead. And so now, I pace the room each night, humming Radiohead songs, to my ever-expanding three-year-old.

The Sainsburys delivery man warned me of this, many moons ago. He spoke of horror stories of his nephew still being rocked to sleep aged six.

"*That will be us*," I thought to myself, whilst agreeably replying "*Oh gosh, that sounds terrible!*"

I try to picture Casey at six. And me aged 40, buckling under his weight, and the image makes me laugh. But then, I could never have imagined that I'd still be rocking a three-year-old to sleep each night.

The strange thing is, he still rests his head in the crook of my neck, just as he did as a newborn. But oh the limbs on my leggy boy can't quite be contained in the same way. Halfway down my body now. Hoisting him back up every so often. Pacing, hoisting, pacing, until he suddenly gets heavier and I know his eyes must have closed over.

For the last week he has uncharacteristically asked to fall asleep whilst lying down in his bed. And so, I sit and stroke his hair awkwardly through the bed guard, and whisper sleep-making stories. Wondering if I'm, in fact, making matters worse by over-faffing. This goes on for an age. And then eventually that little voice concedes:

"Mummy. I want you to rock me."

He only has to ask me the once.

Oh come here, my heavy lump. You are still too small and undeniably cute to refuse.

missing puzzle piece

There was a strange uneasiness in the few years before Casey came along. It would wake me in the night. A niggling feeling. It was as if I always knew I was missing something. Waiting for something. But I could never put my finger on it.

I thought maybe it was because I lacked purpose or ambition. I had jobs but never a calling. Or a single hobby even. I frustrated myself with it. I loved film and music. I was an expert consumer of things. I just didn't really like *doing* anything.

> *"Motherhood. That'll be your thing,"* Spence would say.

It makes me laugh now that we'd casually put motherhood on a par with picking up cross-stitch or trying out yoga. And it really makes me laugh, that we assumed it would be my thing. That I'd sail it.

But, sure enough, that restless feeling disappeared when Casey arrived. Perhaps the busyness of new motherhood put a stop to it. I like to think it's because he was the missing puzzle piece.

And in a round-about way, Spence was right. Motherhood did give me a *thing*. A hobby at long last.

I would jot down notes on my phone in little, stolen moments. In the in-between spaces. Sentences would come to me whilst feeding him to sleep. I'd edit and revise poems by speaking them aloud over and over, whilst pounding the pavements in pursuit of naps.

Words saved me from the temporary madness of early motherhood. I wrote myself out of it.

Spence asked me recently what I wanted for my birthday and I asked for *"A few hours alone, to write."*

the most important work

In no other job have I felt the need to so routinely justify my productivity within a day. To myself.

Because it is mostly myself that this pressure comes from; a silly deep-seated belief that because I'm not earning, because I'm not financially contributing to my household or the wider world, that I am somehow less.

I once had a temp job where I was paid to literally sit and read *Heat* magazine, laugh at my bosses jokes, and look busy if anyone appeared. I felt no guilt about this because I was earning, I was contributing, right?

The thing about the work of motherhood is that it is so difficult to quantify. How do we measure a good day's work anyway? Number of nappies changed? Number of vegetables consumed? Dishes washed? Tantrums dissolved? What is my output? It's often invisible. Jobs get completed then swiftly undone again.

Spence has flippantly remarked before that I "*have it easy*" being the one at home. Then, in the next instant, has said he can't wait to get back to work for a break. So, which one is it?

When will we truly value the *work* of stay at home parents? I guess it starts with me, when I am unapologetically proud of this job.

When I can look back after three years and see not just a huge gaping hole in my CV but rather my defining role, doing the most important work I'll ever do.

puddles

Three days, they said. That magic period of time where you can seemingly master anything; sleep, weaning, potty training.

Well, it's been three *months* of potty training here and some days it feels like we are back to square one.

I'm firm friends with the disinfectant now. We laid our sofa to rest months ago. I live between wees. In the same way that I lived between feeds in the early days. Great, he's just wee'd, that's us good for at least an hour.

Some days are brilliant. He happily takes himself off to the potty then gleefully announces that he has a surprise for me. I am genuinely thrilled. My barometer for delight has changed considerably these days.

Other days, I am drowning in puddles of wee.

This seems to be the nature of motherhood in general. Good day, followed by bad day, followed by good day. Gliding. Then drowning.

As September and nursery approaches, I feel a pressure to have this all sorted. It will be his first time away from me. And it feels like for the first time we'll both be accountable to someone else.

As I kneel down to mop up another puddle, he looks up at me and says:

"Don't worry mum. I'm still just getting used to it."

Me too, love. Me too.

the long game

I accidentally tripped and fell into attachment parenting. I think many mums do. I had never heard of it before. All I knew was that I couldn't relate to the things I read on those mainstream apps or those baby forums and I felt unfathomably alone for it.

In many ways, I'm not the typical attachment mum. I never babywore. We didn't co-sleep, although he was in our room until the age of two.

But increasingly I found solace in breastfeeding groups where mums would ask the questions that were swirling around my head.

A like-minded mum, with a similarly sleepless baby, sent me an article which explained attachment parenting and the benefits of it.

In all honesty, I wasn't initially comforted by it. It felt too hard. It spoke in terms of years rather than months. It seemed like such a long game. With no easy solutions.

But it felt easier than the suggested alternatives, so I stuck it out. I played the long game and in the back of my mind, as sleep continued to regress,

I worried that this might bite me on the bum. That we would never sleep again.

But sure enough, he is approaching three, and *we sleep*. In glorious blocks of five, six, seven, sometimes 11 hours.

And I wish I had soaked up the one-ness of early motherhood. Because it's changing lately. All those once so immediate needs are not so immediate any more. All those fears that I was making a 'clingy' child, now dissipated. All my instincts, once wobbly and questioned, now validated. An independence borne from a dependence that once felt suffocating, but is now missed.

No longer my baby. Never really 'mine' to begin with.

cross that bridge

I've always had a tendency to over prepare. To prevent. To pre-emptively worry things out of existence. As a child, I would sleep all night in my school uniform to save vital minutes in the morning. Because being late for school would have been a fate worse than death.

And motherhood offered up a world of worry.

But overpreparing and worrying in motherhood essentially amounted to wishing it away. To missing the current magic, for fear of failing to prepare for any future misery.

I worried about how we would stop breastfeeding. The worry loomed heavy like a raincloud over the breastfeeding years. I worried that he would never sleep longer than two hours in a row. That he would never fall asleep without boob.

And now that he's three. Now that he finally sleeps and rises sluggishly at 8am and refuses to wear clothes, I worry that we should really *"do something about that."* Because he's going to be starting nursery soon. How will we ever get out the door come September?

And my past self wants to shake my present self. Why can't you see? This is the good bit. The sweet spot. And you're missing it. Grab it. Now. Before you lose him to the world of school.

To hell with your preparedness. It's the summer holidays ffs. In the middle of a worldwide pandemic ffs. Let him sleep until noon. Revel in that glorious slumber that you've dreamt of this entire time. Savour these slow, lazy mornings. Watch all the Scooby Doo and we'll cross that bridge when we get to it. Because when it comes down to it, that's all we ever end up doing anyway.

no more tears

I have actually become Mrs Large, hankering after five minutes peace.

Sure, I can indulge in daytime showers, but they are not what they once were. I offer up bargaining tools; yogurt raisins and bath toys. I accept that all our worldly possessions can, and will be, thrown over the banister.

The snacks appease you for a moment but soon you insist on washing my hair. I dutifully kneel down as you gleefully spray water into my eyes, my ears, my mouth. Everywhere. Anywhere, but onto my actual head.

Once the bathroom is suitably soaked, you ask to come in too. I reach for the non-slip mat and lift you in. You prod at my *"funny tummy"* and protest at the sight of the baby shampoo. So much for 'no more tears.'

You declare that you don't like baths anymore. That you want a shower every day because it feels *"like a waterfall."*

Inevitably, you wee on us both.

I rinse off our feet then step out of the bath, miraculously feeling less clean than when I started.

I momentarily eye up the body moisturiser. Dream on love.

I wrap us both up in a gigantic soggy bath towel. Take one look at your slick combed-back hair and baby face. All is forgiven.

When you start nursery tomorrow, I will be truly squeaky clean for the first time in years. Shaved. Buffed. Moisturised. To within an inch of my life. But I will be side-kick-less.

Gains and losses.

no keeping you

I thought I was afraid of creating a clingy child. Someone who relied on me too heavily, at times suffocatingly, for everything. I thought freedom was what I coveted. An independent child. A strange, impossible concept when you really think about it.

And I worried that I hadn't socialised you enough. Painfully aware that three moves in three years had left us depleted of village and all those regular outside influences that can so benefit a child.

But slowly that number crept upon us. Three.

And so I called the nursery. Arranged a viewing. I felt suddenly ill-prepared, scared that I hadn't done enough. But in you walked; confident, oblivious, hugging the other children, playing happily and not once glancing back in my direction. Just as I finally found my feet, so did you.

And I was proud. But also afraid. Because therein lies the real fear. The very thing I thought we had been striving towards all this time; independence.

Because in that moment, I realised that although you were born mine, there will be no keeping you.

just you wait

I have less to say lately. About being a mum. The rhymes don't come so easy these days.

I've less of those big feelings.
Less tears.
More laughs.
I've started to fancy Spence more.
Music sounds better.
I crack more jokes.
I feel lighter.
And younger.
And more interested in outside things.

All signs, I think, that I'm getting more sleep. Or that this is somehow getting a bit easier.

Everybody said *"Just you wait,"* which I had always interpreted as a threat of worse to come. But perhaps, this is what they meant.

Just you wait.

acknowledgements

A big thank you to Gemma Nunn, for her editing brilliance, and for introducing me to the comma.

A big thank you to Alice Atkinson, for the beautiful cover artwork. Alice is a talented illustrator and mum of three who can be found on Instagram under the alias @this_mama_draws

about the author

Karen McMillan lives in the UK with her partner Spencer and their son, Casey.

She shares poetry and prose online under the alias of Mother Truths on both Instagram and Facebook.

Also by Karen McMillan:

Mother Truths: Poems on Early Motherhood is available to buy on Amazon.

www.ingramcontent.com/pod-product-compliance
Lightning Source LLC
Chambersburg PA
CBHW021445080526
44588CB00009B/698